MW01234688

Medicinal Mushrooms:

15 Mushrooms For Healing Without Pills

Table of Contents

Introduction

For years, our ancestors have been relying on herbs and medicinal mushrooms to cure ailments of different kinds. The modern-day medicines might help you get instant relief, but they also come with plenty of side effects as well.

These days, lots of people are moving to naturopathy and other age-old techniques to keep their body healthy and fit. If you also wish to stay at peace and heal yourself without causing any unwanted side-effect, then you have come to the right place.

In this guide, we will make you familiar with the healing power of various medicinal mushrooms. Additionally, we will also let you know about their composition, the kinds of problems they can cure, and how they should be used.

If you don't have any knowledge about medicinal mushrooms, then don't worry. We will start from the basics and cover everything in detail here. We will also teach you how to pick the right kinds of mushrooms, so that you could differentiate between medicinal and ordinary mushrooms.

Read on and know how medicinal mushrooms can be used to attain a perfect body and mind.

Chapter 1 – Health Benefits Of Mushrooms

Mushrooms have been associated with good health for a very long time. Though, just like any other shrub, mushrooms can also be of different kinds. There are times when people simply generalize mushrooms as being poisonous. While there are a few toxic species of mushrooms in the world, one can also find mushrooms with high medicinal properties as well.

Therefore, before you proceed, make sure that you stay focused and keep only medicinal mushrooms in your mind. Just like we need to differentiate healthy shrubs from the poisonous ones, try to do the same with mushrooms as well.

Don't worry! Later in this guide, we will teach you how to recognize toxic mushrooms as well. Nevertheless, it is important to know the health benefits that are associated with mushrooms beforehand.

It is a noted fact that mushrooms have some of the most nutritive and medicinal properties that exist in nature. More than 100 different species of mushrooms are considered medicinal and were already used by our ancestors. Though, out of this lot, some of the species are considered extremely healthy and significant for our body.

A few mushrooms can strengthen our immune system and can even regulate our blood pressure. According to plenty of recent studies, mushrooms can act as a muscle relaxer, improve our vitamin D level, boost our immunity, provide essential nutrients, and has lots of other medicinal benefits.

Some of the mushroom species have a medicinal compound, known as *Cordyceps*. It has recently been identified as a cancer drug and can help thousands of cancer patients the world over to get better. A few other problems like asthma, renal failure, strokes, arthritis, hepatitis, diabetes, etc. can also be cured by mushrooms.

Additionally, you must know that only natural mushrooms have medicinal properties. Organic mushrooms absorb essential nutrients from the soil (or wood logs). These kinds of medicinal properties can't be found in artificially grown products. Turkey Tail, Reishi, Shiitake, Maitake, and Chaga are some of the commonly found medicinal mushrooms.

Following are some of the noted medicinal benefits of mushrooms:

- Mushrooms can balance your entire diet. They have a high content of vitamins and nutrients that should definitely be consumed by all of us.

- If you wish to lose weight, then you can consume white button mushrooms. In place of meat, if you eat mushrooms, then you might end up shredding a lot of weight. It will let you have a balanced diet while getting rid of those extra pounds.

- Finding an ideal natural substitute of vitamin D is quite hard. Luckily, in white mushrooms, scientists have found a significant amount of Vitamin D2 and D3. If you have vitamin D deficiency, then you should definitely include mushrooms in your diet.

- It has been discovered that mushrooms have alpha and beta glucan molecules, which can boost our immune system to a great extent. By adding a handful of shiitake mushroom in your diet, you can strengthen the overall immune efficiency of your body.

- Parasitic mushrooms like Tochukasu are known to have anti-ageing properties. They are even used by athletes to boost endurance and strength.

- Not just to boost our physical characteristics, a few species are known to have hypoglycemic properties and can be used as an antidepressant as well.

- Some medicinal mushrooms are known to treat diseases like Hepatitis B.

- A regular dosage of healthy mushrooms can normalize our body's cholesterol level and increase our blood flow.

- Most recently, parasitic fungi have been evolved to become a cancer drug as well.

With so many amazing benefits, how can one say no to these medicinal mushrooms?

They can help you live a long and healthy life for sure. Now when you are aware of their general benefits, let's proceed and know how to consume them in the next chapter.

Chapter 2 – Medicinal Mushrooms Preparation & Consumption

Some of the mushrooms have such amazing medicinal properties that they were even associated with the harbinger of immortality in stories. Though, in order to consume the right kind of mushrooms, it is important to know how they are prepared as well. We have listed some of the common techniques that you can implement to prepare and consume mushrooms of different kinds.

Soup Broth

This is one of the most ideal ways of consuming mushrooms. Whenever you are feeling bad, just make a healing broth and shred mushrooms like Reishi in it. Though, while making a broth, make sure that you put mushrooms in an ideal quantity. Majorly, the quantity of the mushroom used depends on its type and species.

Hot tea

For years, people have been adding medicinal mushrooms while preparing hot tea. Most of the mushrooms have a woody and tough exterior. By boiling them in water, you can break down their exterior, letting them dissolve the quantities in the water.

Ideally, you can use a handful of mushrooms per liter. Now, boil the mixture for another 15-20 minutes. If you want to increase the efficiency, then you can let the mixture simmer for even an hour. Also, you can combine other herbs like ginger or basil in the mix. Consume the tea when hot to maximize the effect.

Tincture

The alcohol tinctures of mushrooms can also be used to extract the medicinal properties out of them. To make it, fill almost half of a jar with pieces of mushrooms. Now, fill it with alcohol to the top. Make sure that at least half of the jar is filled with alcohol.

Let this mixture rest like this for another two weeks or so. You can also keep this mixture in a closed jar outside as well. When the tincture is ready, just strain the mushrooms out and prepare its tea. Bottle it up again and consume it whenever you want.

Extract Powder

These days, due to technological advancements, we are able to make extract powders of almost every natural ingredient. Mushrooms are no such exception as well. You can readily buy a natural extract powder of your preferred kind of mushroom or can prepare one yourself.

Simply dry a handful of mushrooms and grind them to make their powder. Later, you can use this powder in the usual way. You can even add it to drinks or just sprinkle it over soups or any other dish of your choice.

It is pretty convenient and will help you maintain the overall balance in your meal without compromising its taste.

Mushroom chocolate

As surprising as it might sound, one can easily make medicinal mushroom chocolates as well. If you want your kids to consume medicinal mushrooms, then this would be a great idea. To start with, prepare the following mixture:

- 1 part cocoa butter

- 2 parts cocoa paste

- 1 part maple syrup (or any other sweetener for your taste)

- 3 tablespoons of mushroom extracts

Now, melt the cocoa butter and mix all the other ingredients. Let it boil for a few minutes until it would turn into a thick paste. When it is done, pour it into a dish and freeze the mix for at least an hour. After when the chocolate would set, break it into pieces and store it to use it afterward.

Simply prepare the mushroom in your desired way and consume it as per your needs. Now when you know how to prepare a mushroom dish, let's move ahead and know more about various species of mushrooms in detail.

Chapter 3 – Essential Medicinal Mushrooms

You might already know that there are different kinds of medicinal mushrooms that are available in the market. You can readily get them from an organic shop or can even grow a few mushroom species at your place as well. Start by getting familiar with these medicinal mushrooms.

Shiitake (Lentinula edodes)

Shiitake is undoubtedly one of the most widely known medicinal mushrooms, which is presently known to mankind. It has a high level of vitamin C, vitamin B2, Iron, and Calcium. After the commonly known button mushroom, it is the second most widely grown mushroom in the world. It is originated from East Asia and is extensively used in traditional Chinese and Thai medicines.

Uses: Shiitake is known for its immune-boosting properties. Since it has anti-virus and anti-tumor characteristics, it can even cure dreadful diseases like cancer. According to a study, it can even diminish the growth of the HIV virus. Additionally, if you have any kind of allergy, flu, or unstable blood pressure, then it can be cured by Shiitake.

Growth: Finding Shiitake is pretty easy. It is mostly found on the top layer of fallen trees of maple, oak, walnut, chestnut, etc. Mostly, it is not easily recognized by novices. Therefore, it is grown by organic farmers in the country. You can easily find fresh shiitake at any leading grocery store.

Consumption: Most of the people usually find the taste of Shiitake pretty good. Therefore, it can be consumed in different ways. You can simply add it to your salads when it is fresh or can make its broth as well.

Reishi (Ganoderma lucidum)

Also known as the Lingzhi mushroom (in China), it is considered as one of the healthiest and medicinal mushrooms in East Asia. It has plenty of varieties as well and its first use has been found documented way back in the 400 BC.

Uses: Reishi has plenty of health benefits. It is used to prepare healthy tonics and is known to calm anxiety. It has anti-viral and anti-allergic properties as well and can be used to treat diseases like Hepatitis. Additionally, it is used as an antidote for poisonous mushrooms as well. If you feel weakness, restlessness, or suffer from insomnia, then you should definitely consume this medicinal mushroom.

Growth: Since Reishi is one of the most popular mushrooms in the world, it is grown in various parts of different continents. It is majorly found in East and Central Asia, the eastern coast of the United States, Europe, and South America. It is also found in the wild and is pretty affordable as well.

Consumption: There are several variations of Reishi and almost every kind of it can be taken in different ways. It can be added to any dish when it is fresh. You can also prepare its tea or an extract powder.

Turkey Tail (Trametes versicolor)

Turkey Tail can be easily found in the wild. The fungi mushroom can also be grown at home, as it can flourish rapidly without much trouble. It doesn't demand strict conditions for its growth as well. The upper surface has concentric zones of different colors, which makes it easier for people to identify it.

Uses: Since it is anti-oxidant properties, it is used to cure plenty of ailments. It is also used by patients suffering from high cholesterol level. Furthermore, it is also used to boost the immunity level of our body.

Growth: Turkey Tail has recently seen a massive growth and is easily found worldwide. Its different variants can be seen in parts of China, Europe, and the United States. In the wild, it can be seen flourishing on dead logs.

Consumption: Most of the users prepare its tea in order to consume it in an ideal way. Though, you can also make its soup or simply chew it raw to maximize its effect.

Chaga (Inonotus obliquus)

This parasite mushroom has been originated from Russia and is also associated with traditional European medicines. Since it is mostly found in cold habitats, growing it at your home is pretty tough. Recently, a study has found that Chaga can drastically help cancer patients. This has brought a major change in the way people consume this medicinal mushroom.

Uses: For years, Chaga has been an essential part of traditional Russian medicines. It is a natural pain reliever and can also purify our blood. It has been discovered recently that Chaga also has anti-tumor and anti-cancer properties.

Growth: Unlike most of the other mushrooms, this one can't be grown easily in a tropical climate. It is mostly grown in Alaska, Eastern United States, Europe, and other cold regions. It has a stalk-less growth and its black color makes it pretty evident to be discovered. Mostly, it grows on birch, alder, or elm.

Consumption: One of the easiest ways to consume it is by preparing its tea. Though, people also ferment it or make its tincture. You can find its natural extract at a leading store as well, which can be used in different ways.

Maitake (Grifola frondosa)

This edible fungus is native to China and for ages, it has been associated with traditional Chinese and Japanese medicines. The name translates to "dancing mushroom" in Japanese. It was so precious in the ancient times that people used to exchange it with the same weight in silver.

Uses: Maitake has plenty of uses. Most commonly, it is used to control blood pressure and regulate the cholesterol level in our body. It is also used as an anti-depressant by many. The mushroom also has anti-cancer properties, making it a part of a breakthrough research. Due to its diverse usage, it is also known as "king of mushrooms" in Japan.

Growth: Earlier, Maitake was found only in parts of China and Japan. Today, due to its amazing medicinal properties, it has found its way in other parts of the world like Europe, Central Asia, and the Americas as well.

Consumption: One can simply prepare its broth or can even make its tea to use it readily. If you want to use it in the long run, then you can make its powder as well.

Oyster (Pleurotus ostreatus)

The mushroom was originally grown in Germany during World War I for subsistence measure. Gradually, it gained immense popularity due to its health benefits and is presently considered as one of the most widely used fungi of all. It has a high content of iron, manganese, vitamin B1, B2, and amino acids. It has a distinctive shell-like structure which also looks like an oyster.

Uses: The mushroom can be used to create a balanced and nutritive diet. It also regulates the level of cholesterol in our body. It acts as an excellent muscle relaxant as well.

Growth: It was originally grown in Germany and widely flourished in other parts of Europe as well. Today, its commercial production takes place in America, Asia, and other European countries.

Consumption: Most of the times, it is pretty hard to find a fresh oyster mushroom. Therefore, people prepare its extract or make its capsules. You can always make its broth if you find a fresh oyster.

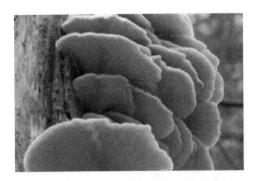

Cordyceps (Cordyceps sinensis)

This medicinal mushroom was originally discovered in the Tibetan plateau and has gradually flourished in other parts of Asia as well. It is known to boost our immune system and kill cancer-causing cells in our body. Spotting this medicinal mushroom is quite easy. Mostly, it doesn't have a shell. Instead, it has a saffron shade and is erected without a cap.

Uses: Cordyceps has plenty of benefits. It cleans our blood and acts as a natural anti-cancer agent. Additionally, it boosts our immune system with its virus-fighting ability.

Growth: Though the mushroom was originally cultivated in Tibet, it gradually became popular in other parts of the world as well. Today, it is commercially grown in Thailand, Japan, India, and other Asian countries.

Consumption: One of the best ways to consume it is by making a hot tea or broth. If you are in the US or Europe, then chances are that you might not find it fresh. Therefore, you can also buy its natural extract as well.

Lion's Mane (Hericium erinaceus)

It is also known as pom-pom or bearded tooth mushroom by many, due to its distinctive appearance. It is pretty easy to identify Lion's Mane, as it has long white spikes instead of a shell. From forests to beaches, it is found in different parts all over the world during late summer.

Uses: It has high protein content and is even used for garnishing in many cuisines as well. Lion's Mane has two crucial components - hericenones and erinacines. These components are scientifically proven to boost our nervous system. A daily dose of this medicinal mushroom can boost your brain activity and strengthen your nervous system. It is also used to treat strokes, seizures, dementia, and other cognitive neural disorders.

Growth: The mushroom is associated with Native America and is found growing in its natural way at plenty of American beaches. It is also grown in China, Japan, and other Asian countries.

Consumption: One can simply garnish their dishes with it or even add flavor to a cuisine by adding its natural extract. It can be eaten fresh as well.

Agaricus (Agaricus brasiliensis)

This Brazilian mushroom is also known as "Cogumelo do sol" by the natives. People also call it mushroom of the sun or almond mushroom, as it tastes similar to almonds. This edible mushroom is known to mankind for decades and is used to boost our immune system.

Uses: It has been discovered that Agaricus has anti-cancer and anti-tumor properties. It is also used as a replacement for chemotherapy in plenty of Asian countries. The mushroom is also used to increase our body's immunity.

Growth: The mushroom is found in abundance in Northern and Central America. Originated from Brazil, it is also commercially grown in European and Asian countries as well.

Consumption: Unlike most of the other mushrooms, this one is soaked in hot water or alcohol to prepare a mixture. You can either consume the mixture or eat it raw.

Agarikon (Laricifomes officinalis)

This ancient mushroom is presently used to make different modern medicines. It has a distinctive woody appearance and a bitter taste. It has a complete spectrum of myco-nutrients, which makes it one of the healthiest mushrooms of all.

Uses: If you want to attain a balanced diet, then you should definitely add Agarikon to your meals. It has beneficial compounds such as glucans, ergosterols, glycoproteins, and more. A latest research has discovered that the mushroom also has anti-viral properties and can be used to make plenty of modern drugs.

Growth: The first documented use of Agarikon was found in the 65 AD by the Ancient Greeks. Today, the mushroom is grown globally in different countries. Though, its color changes from one place to another. It can be of yellow-white to dark brown, depending on the location.

Consumption: The best way to consume it is by making its tea in hot water. You can also add it with other ingredients to make a fresh broth.

Enokitake (Flammulina velutipes)

This long, thin, and white mushroom has been associated with East Asian cuisines for ages. It is also known as the gold needle mushroom or the lily mushroom by many. It usually grows in dense forests around winter.

Uses: The mushroom is considered as a source of high protein. It has anti-toxic and cardiotoxic protein characteristics and is used as a natural blood cleanser. It is also used to strengthen our immune system and to make medicines for cancer immunotherapy.

Growth: The mushroom is mostly found in Asian countries like China, Japan, Thailand, and Vietnam. Gradually, it is crossing the bridge and many western countries have also started its organic farming.

Consumption: One can create a tincture of this mushroom with alcohol and use it in the future. Also, it can be consumed fresh to create broths.

Mesima (Phellinus linteus)

It is also known as the "black hoof mushroom" in Native America and "song gen" in China. It has a bitter taste and is identified by its distinctive hoof like shape.

Uses: Mesima is used to balance the hormonal changes in our body. It is also used to cure Type-2 diabetes. It has been discovered that Mesima has anti-cancer properties and is particularly used to treat patients with breast cancer.

Growth: Mesima is grown in Northern America, China, and Korea. It is mostly found growing on the mulberry trees.

Consumption: You can eat this mushroom in its raw form or can make a hot tea by including other ingredients like ginger and honey.

Artist's Conk (Ganoderma applanatum)

Also known as an artist's bracelet, it is a bracelet fungus which grows in different parts of the world. The fungus can sometimes be as long as 30-50 centimeters at times. It has been a part of the traditional Asian medicine for years.

Uses: The mushroom has anti-bacterial, anti-virus, and anti-fibrotic properties. Due to this, it is used to treat different kinds of ailments. It is even used to make cancer-curing medicines as well.

Growth: The mushroom is commercially grown in Europe, United States, China, Japan, and different other nations. Its unique shape makes it quite easy to be recognized by people. It mostly grows on trees like oak, maple, chestnut, apple, willow, walnut, etc.

Consumption: Most of the times, people makes a natural extract and use it as per their requirements. You can also prepare its tincture or use a part of it to make tea.

Ice Man Mushroom (Fomes fomentarius)

It is a natural parasite and decomposer that usually grows on dead trees. This medicinal mushroom is almost 5000 years old and has a prominent hoof-shape. It has a distinctive range of colors from silver to black (sometimes, it can be of dark brown as well).

Uses: It is used to improve digestion and has anti-inflammatory properties. Additionally, it has been discovered that the mushroom has anti-viral characteristics. It has been a part of the ancient Roman and Chinese medicines for a long time.

Growth: The mushroom is found in plenty of places in Asia, America, Europe, and Africa. Since it is a natural decomposer, it is found growing on dead and decayed trees.

Consumption: Its most ideal form of consumption is either hot tea or broth. Nevertheless, if you can't find the mushroom in its raw form, then you can always buy is natural extract powder.

Birch Polypore (Piptoporus betulinus)

This bracelet mushroom is produced globally due to its prominent health benefits. Not just that, it is also used for culinary purposes these days. This edible mushroom has a strong and desirable odor with a bitter taste. It is estimated to be as old as 5000 years.

Uses: The medicinal mushroom has anti-virus properties and is used to cure a common cold and flu. It is also used to provide a boost to our immune system, as it is a great source of essential nutrients.

Growth: The mushroom is grown in Europe, America, Asia, and plenty of other nations all over the world.

Consumption: One can use the mushroom for garnishing purposes as well. Simply make its broth or a hot tea by adding other ingredients. You can get this mushroom readily from any leading store as well.

Besides the above-mentioned list, there are plenty of other mushrooms as well that one can use. Some of the popular ones are Yun Zhi (Trametes versicolor), Oregon Polypore (Ganoderma oregonense), Suehirotake (Schizophyllum commune), Zhu Ling (Polyporus umbellatus), and more.

We have listed some of the most commonly found and essential medicinal mushrooms that everyone should be aware of. You can easily get these mushrooms from an organic store nearby. Nevertheless, if you want to grow your own mushrooms, then read on. We have presented a quick guide about it in the next section.

Chapter 4 – Grow Your Own Medicinal Mushrooms At Home

This might surprise you, but you can grow some of the most common medicinal mushrooms at the convenience of your home. While most of the above-mentioned mushrooms are farmed commercially, a handful of them like Shiitake, Maitake, Reishi, and more can easily be grown at home.

By maintaining an ideal environment, it becomes pretty easy to grow these mushrooms and allowing them to propagate organically. To do this, you can simply follow these steps.

Select the spawns

As you might already know, in order to grow an entire colony of mushrooms, you need to start by selecting the spawn. You can ideally visit a forest to handpick spawns or can simply buy them at a leading store as well.

To start with, you need to mist it with water every day. Spawns are sold in sawdust, grain, and other mediums as well. After getting the appropriate spawn, you should transfer it to a sustaining medium as soon as possible.

Growing the mushrooms

Almost every kind of medicinal mushroom gets nutrients from its medium (soil, wood log, etc.) in order to grow. Since most of the mushrooms sustain on an organic or decaying matter, growing them at home requires an extra effort.

To start with, consider a wood log as an ideal medium to grow mushrooms. While there are plenty of other mediums as well, wood logs are considered the most preferred ones. We have listed various measures you should take to grow these famous kinds of mushrooms.

Shiitake: This smoky flavored mushroom is usually grown on the bark of trees like alder, oak, ironwood, maple, and more. You can simply place a log of these trees in the temperate range of 60-80 degree Fahrenheit. Though, patience is the key here. You might have to wait for 6 months to two years in order to yield its growth.

Lion's Mane: Lion's Mane is known for its unique appearance with clusters of combs that can be as long as 1-2 centimeters. To grow this medicinal mushroom, maintain a temperate of 60 to 70 degree Fahrenheit and let them propagate on wood logs of aspen, maple, or oak.

Oyster: Growing oyster at home is comparatively easier than other mushrooms. To start with, get a wood log of trees like aspen, willow, elm, balsam poplar, cottonwood, or basswood. Maintain the temperature of 50 to 70 degree Fahrenheit and wait for a few months for the colony to propagate.

Reishi: This medicinal Chinese mushroom has a bitter taste and is mostly grown on logs of sugar maple or oak, when kept at a temperature of 60 to 80 degree Fahrenheit.

Maitake: It is also known as "hen of the wood" and has a feather-like look. Maintain a temperature of 55 to 70 degree Fahrenheit and place your spawns over a damp log of chestnut or oak to grow Maitake.

Sometimes, people have to dig holes in the wood log and place the spawns in order to have a sustaining colony of mushrooms.

Make sure that the wood log is at least 2-4 feet long, so that the mushrooms can grow without much trouble. Maintain high humidity and the respective temperature range in order to grow these medicinal mushrooms at home.

How to identify toxic mushrooms?

If you are out in the wild while looking for medicinal mushrooms, then chances are that you might end up picking a toxic mushroom as well. Keep the following things in mind while selecting a mushroom.

1. If the shell of the mushroom has white gills, then avoid it. Most of these mushrooms are poisonous.

2. Also, avoid the mushroom if its stem has a ring or a skirt-like structure.

3. If the mushroom has a red cap, then it should not be picked. Lots of toxic mushrooms have a red stem or cap.

4. Most of the mushrooms that are grown on wood logs are considered safe (besides a few exceptions).

5. Only pick the kind of mushrooms that you are able to recognize. You can easily take the assistance of technology and search the picture of the mushroom on the web to identify its nature.

Now when you know how to handpick the right kinds of mushroom, you would certainly be able to get medicinal mushrooms during your next trip. Additionally, by following the above-listed instructions, you can easily grow your own mushrooms at home.

Go ahead and give it a try. Say goodbye to all those drugs and heal your body naturally by taking the assistance of these medicinal mushrooms.

Conclusion

Congratulations for finishing the guide so soon. We are sure you must have had a great experience learning the benefits of various medicinal mushrooms. If you wish to stop taking modern medicines or drugs, then you can easily rely on mushrooms as a healthy substitute.

For years, our ancestors have been using medicinal mushrooms to cure various ailments and diseases. Not just to cure flu or fever, they can also be used to cure serious diseases like cancer, hepatitis, or diabetes.

In this guide, we have made you familiar with various ways of consuming mushrooms along with their health benefits. Furthermore, we discussed some of the commonly found medicinal mushrooms in detail, including their uses, consumption, growth, etc.

You can easily get most of these medicinal mushrooms at an organic shop. Nevertheless, if you wish to grow them on your own, then you can follow our simple instructions or research regarding the species of mushrooms you want to grow.

In the end, we have also provided some simple instructions that you should follow while picking medicinal mushrooms in the wild. We are sure that this will keep you away from any toxic substance.

So what are you waiting for? Go ahead and prepare a hot tea or a delicious broth of a few medicinal mushrooms and bring a much-needed change to your health.

FREE Bonus Reminder

If you have not grabbed it yet, please go ahead and download your special bonus report *"DIY Projects. 13 Useful & Easy To Make DIY Projects To Save Money & Improve Your Home!"*

Simply Click the Button Below

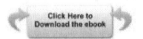

OR **Go to This Page**

http://diyhomecraft.com/free

BONUS #2: More Free & Discounted Books or Products

Do you want to receive more Free/Discounted Books or Products?

We have a mailing list where we send out our new Books or Products when they go free or with a discount on Amazon. Click on the link below to sign up for Free & Discount Book & Product Promotions.

=> Sign Up for Free & Discount Book & Product Promotions <=

OR Go to this URL

http://bit.ly/1WBb1Ek

Made in the USA
Coppell, TX
02 July 2024

34204213R00020